A Way Out
FROM DARKNESS TO LIGHT

POEMS AND TESTIMONIES OF GOD'S GRACE FROM SURVIVORS OF SEX TRAFFICKING

Casondra Nichole Austin
Maria Claire
Leah Gunn
Iris Socorro Santiago
Kelsea Brooke Vaughn

A Way Out: From Darkness to Light

KDP Publishing, Independent Publishing Platform, Printed in the United States of America

Copyright © 2020 by A Way Out Ministries, P.O. Box 770775, Memphis, TN 38177
Cover Designed by: Leah Gunn and Brian Borgman

All rights reserved. For permission requests, write to the author, at: www.awoministries.org

1. 2 Corinthians 5:7, NASB
2. Matthew 16:23, NIV
3. Celebration Road Show & Newton, J. (1970) Amazing Grace Hymn. Celebration Records, United States.
4. Zechariah 4:6, KJV
5. Isaiah 61:3, KJV
6. Romans 8:1, KJV
7. 1 John 4:18, ESV
8. Isaiah 40:31, ESV
9. John 8:32, NIV
10. Isaiah 53:5, NIV
11. Revelation 12;11, NASB
12. Psalm 27:13, NIV
13. Esther 4:14, NIV

Verses marked NIV are taken from the HOLY BIBLE NEW INTERNATIONAL VERSION ®. NIV®. Copyright © 1973, 1978, 1984, 2011 by International Bible Society. Used by permission of Zondervan Publishing House. All Rights Reserved. Verses marked NASB are taken from the New American Standard Bible®, Copyright © 1960, 1962, 1963, 1968, 1971, 1972, 1973, 1975, 1977, 1995 by The Lockman Foundation. Used by permission. Verses marked KJV are taken from the King James Version of the Bible. Verses marked ESV are taken from The Holy Bible, English Standard Version, copyright © 2001 by Crossway Bibles, a division of Good News Publishers. Used by permission. All rights reserved.

ISBN 978-1-7345543-0-4
e-Book ISBN 978-1-7345543-1-1

Casondra

Iris

Kelsea

LEAH

2019

All in 2 way Out

DEDICATION

As your sisters who have received freedom through Christ, we dedicate this book to all those still trapped in
human trafficking and to all the future women who will find a safe place to be restored at A Way Out.

Cathy Graham, you were the first person to hear the vision for this book, and instead of discouraging me, you provided everything financially possible to make this book a reality. You had faith and believed in us from the very start.

Kaitrin Valencia, thank you so much for teaching us what needed to be done, spending so much time getting the book from a notebook onto the computer, formatting, and loving us through our impatience.

Luke Lindemann, thank you for being so honest about changes that needed to be made. You have taught us so much about poetry! You spent great lengths of time answering all of our random questions and showing us exactly what, and how to improve the book.

Charlie Sanders, thank you for proofreading and for all of your wonderful advice. I had so much fun during our photo session! I was so sad when it wouldn't upload, it would have made an amazing cover!

Barbara E. McCain, thank you for proofing our book and sharing your sweet feedback. You encouraged us in such a special way.

A Way Out family, you are the hands and feet of Jesus for us ladies. We are so blessed that God chose us to be here and grow with each of you by our side.

Carol Martin, thank you for the fun photoshoot!

Brian Borgman, you are a very talented graphic designer! You took Leah's idea and made it a reality for us! We will forever be grateful!

There are many more people that helped and encouraged us along the way. Thank you from the bottom of our hearts.

TABLE OF CONTENTS

Dedication

Foreword

Introduction

Casondra Nichole Austin

About the Vision

Vision for "A Way Out"

Think It's A Game

They are Following Me

Carried Away

Relief

Loaded Gun

Behind the Mask

Crying Out

I Will Show You

Read

Healing

Word of God

Walk by Faith

Mother's Day 2019

Much Greater

Restore

Invade My Senses

Brand New World

Kelsea Brooke Vaughn

Seek Him

Refuse to Sink

Invited

Iris Socorro Santiago

Reaching Out

I'm Ready, Get Set, Let's Go

1, 2, 3 Welcome to the Deep

What Do You See

Maria Claire

Bitter Wounds

Leah Gunn

Heavy Hand

Tears of Terror

Wrong Time – Wrong Place

My Spree

My Bunk is Hard

Toe to Toe

Heavenly Hope

Indeed

The Heist

Doing Life

You Gotta Hate That Sin

Meet The Authors

FOREWORD

It is with great honor that I write the foreward to this raw and authentic book of poetry authored by five courageous women who've exited the sex trafficking industry.

Ranging from ages 19 to 54, each of these five women have overcome unimaginable challenges "by the blood of the Lamb and the word of [their] testimony." Revelation 12:11

This is not a traditional, "feel good" book. These are raw real accounts from human trafficking survivors' inmost depths. The women represent a unique segment of our society in the United States – rural, small town, urban, Hispanic, Caucasian, young, middle aged, older, trafficked by strangers, boyfriends, husbands, and yes even family members.

As an advocate for over two decades, I can attest there is unfortunately nowhere to hide from this atrocity. It knows no bounds of age, race, or economic status. It exposes the darkest of humanity.

Yet out of the darkness LIGHT shines. These woman surrendered their pain, surrendered their anger, and surrendered their lives to Jesus. And now a new story has emerged. A redemptive story. A story of beauty. A story of forgiveness. A story of purpose.

The best part is, by purchasing their book you are partnering with them in writing this new story. You are literally helping support a survivor in their journey to find freedom. How?

The tenacious women who authored this book graciously donated all sales to sow back into the very program that helped them find a way out of human trafficking. All the revenue generated will help future women find the same freedom through A Way Out Ministries. Thank you for sowing into good soil!

As you enter into their gut-wrenching realities, I want to challenge you to engage and be disturbed. Disturbed to the point of getting involved in the fight to end human trafficking. With revelation comes responsibility. I promise when you engage, your life will never be the same. Each one of these women and others who have survived unthinkable trauma have impacted and changed my life. Pray, volunteer, sow.

Kaitrin E. Valencia, Esq.
Author & Executive Director
A Way Out Ministries

INTRODUCTION

The poems in this book were written by women who have been or are still participants in The A Way Out Program. AWO is a two-year residential recovery program for women who have been exploited in the Commercial Sex Industry, namely sex trafficking. This program is the ministry arm of Citizens for Community Values, which was formed as a 501(c)3 in 1992. The founding vision was to advocate for a standard of decency in the Greater Memphis Area by informing citizens of the harms of pornography to children and families and of the effects of the sexually oriented businesses on communities and businesses.

In the process of monitoring the activity in the sexual oriented businesses, it was discovered that there were not only laws being broken, but there were many young women being exploited in these clubs. What we have realized over the years is this: We started helping trafficked women before we knew to call it trafficking. There was no definition of trafficking to help us label what we were fighting. We just knew the darkness of this lifestyle was hurting women and children. Therefore, it was easy for us to decide that if we were going to fight against the harms perpetrated by the commercial sex industry, we also were going to have to help these vulnerable, broken, wounded, and exploited women and their children. The ministry to rescue and restore the vulnerable started with a handful of women reaching out to these girls as they would meet them or as they would call for help. Originally, help came as volunteers sought pro bono services or asked individuals to help financially for specific needs.
The work continued in a very grassroots manner until 1999,

when Carolyn McKenzie, the Founder, needed to retire and CCV hired an Executive Director, George Kuykendall. In 2000, they decided to hire someone with a counseling background to develop a structured program for the victims. They hired Carol Wiley, who came on staff to accomplish this task. The program she developed was named A Way Out. For the first 10 years CCV/AWO was run with a staff of two and many volunteers. As staff was added, the services expanded and in 2015, George retired and Russ White was hired as Executive Director. Today CCV/AWO operates with four full-time and one part-time member. We are still very dependent on many volunteers and ministry partners, who work together with staff to make sure the women's needs are met as they work the program under the direction of Carol Wiley. In 2019 CCV was rebranded and is now doing business as A Way Out Ministries. The A Way Out Program remains the ministry arm under this new umbrella. The vision and outreach are still to rescue and restore those caught up in the darkness of the commercial sex industry.

It will help you to better understand the journey out of darkness these brave poets took, if you understand their two years in The A Way Out Program. They came from jail, the street, and pimps to live in the program safe house and attend classes dealing with issues stemming from the abuse and exploitation they experienced in the industry, and gain job and life skills. All their needs are met to enable them to focus on healing, and recovery. They receive food, clothing, hygiene products, medical and dental services and counseling at no cost to them. All their transportation needs are provided by staff and volunteers. They are helped with fines, and taken to court appearances with an advocate when needed. They also are given a trained Christian mentor who becomes their friend and encourager throughout the program. This friendship often lasts long after they graduate the program. They are given an opportunity for on the job training two afternoons a week through a partnership with a social enterprise, where they learn to make and ship candles.

AWO is Christ-centered and based on the Isaiah 61:1-4. Two foundational beliefs are 1) that we are all created in the image of God with a dignity that no one has a right to touch and 2) there is no permanent change in a life apart from having a living, growing relationship with the Lord Jesus Christ. Therefore, in addition to dealing with their physical, mental, emotional and social issues, the program addresses their spiritual needs through a weekly Bible study and encouraging the women to become active in a church of their choice.

The A Way Out Program has helped over 650 women in varying degrees over the years through this faith- based program. There have been many successes and of course, there have been heart-breaks along the way too. But God has been faithful to change many lives! Over the years it has become very obvious that these young women were not only very hurt and broken, but they were also full of potential and many had special giftings. Many of them have worked through their devastating circumstances by journaling, writing stories and poetry.

I am very grateful to this group of precious women, who got together and decided they want to give back to A Way Out for the help they had received. As you read these poems you will discover as I have over the years that the enemy tried to destroy each of these women, starting when they were very young. I believe with my whole heart that he recognized the potential in each of them and wanted to destroy it before it could be developed and used in God's Kingdom for His glory. What better scheme could he concoct than to start destroying them as children with neglect, abuse, and rejection by the very ones who should keep them safe and love them. This start in life taught them to how to survive in the world by any means available instead of learning to live in the light of the love, acceptance and forgiveness of Christ. Their life experiences became the catalysts for many bad choices as they pursued survival.

Praise God! You will see that the enemy lost because, God had set his affections on these precious women before the foundation of the world. Therefore, He rescued them out of surviving in darkness and exploitation and transferred them into the marvelous light of His grace, mercy, forgiveness and love. We at the A Way Out Program are humbled and blessed to have a small part in helping them learn to live in the light of a growing relationship with Christ and to see their gifts blossom as God heals them.

This book of poetry is their journey from devastation in the depths of darkness to a life of victory in His Kingdom. I thank God for each of them and I thank Him for calling me to walk with them in their journey to become overcomers. It is my hope that as you read their words, you will walk along with them, and also better understand God's redeeming love through their poetry.

Carol Wiley, BAC, Director,
The A Way Out Program

ABOUT THE VISION

My name is Casondra and as I write this vision, I am a resident in a life-changing program, A Way Out Program, that helps restore women who have a background of being trafficked. There are currently five women in the program and on May 30, 2019 as I was working on one of my classes (Experiencing God), God began to press on my heart the vision for this book.

We are five women on a journey to healing.

God has provided and shown Himself to be mighty to each of us, and He is teaching us to hear Him and respond. We are so excited to share our journey and our deepest thoughts throughout the radical transformation from darkness to light.

Not only is this a test of good faith, but also a way we can give back to the non-profit organization that has helped change our lives. We have donated our work for all the book proceeds to go towards the very program that helped us. I am honored that God chose us to start a tradition that we pray can be carried out for years to come with future residents!

May this be Volume One of many more volumes of freedom to come.

Casondra Nichole Austin

God's Story of Redemption through Casondra Nichole Austin

God is within her, she will not fail;

God will help her at break of day.

Psalm 46:5, NIV

Vision for "A Way Out"

Braced to do the impossible
My God, He is unstoppable

Provision from every direction
Just the right selection

This gift bestowed unto me
A vision clear to see

Chosen for victory
Thankful unto Thee

The least of all the vessels
His purpose, I said yes y'all

Held to high esteem
Blessed to be a part of this dream

Victory is in His Name
Heaven from which He came

You get all glory
Without You there is no story

Written by: Casondra Nichole Austin

Think it's a? GaME

Think It's a Game

Think it's a game with your back against the wall
Persecuting and lying, living like Saul.

Think it's a game with a needle in your arm
Begging and pleading to do yourself harm.

Think it's a game when no one's left to hear,
Wishing you were dead while you're drowning in your beer.

Think it's a game with a gun against your head,
All because you got courage and "no" is what you said.

Think it's a game with a knife cutting your wrist,
Crying out: Can anyone see this s**t?

Think it's a game when you bury your baby girl,
Yelling and blaming God, for your heart is tore.

Think it's a game when he beats you half to death,
Believing that he is the only one that you have left.

Think it's a game using your body just to live,
Only for money, never again will you just give.

Think it's a game being left out on the street,
Nowhere to go, because to them you steal and cheat.

Think it's a game when your family won't answer the phone
Abandonment becomes reality, truly alone.

Think it's a game shooting and barely miss,
Then he beat you with the gun, because he was pissed.

Think it's a game when they take your kids away,
And knowing deep down that they are safer this way.

Think it's a game at checkout time, time to go.
Knowing that to survive, you will have to hoe.

Think it's a game when you are burning in hell,
Why this soul did I try to sell?

Think it's a game spitting in God's face,
Yet still His love.. I taste.

Written by: Casondra Austin

My Story ; didn't End

your life matters

They Are Following Me

Stuck in this tangled web
Far from appealing
Unraveling the mess I made
Only by self-dealing

My own mania runs rapid
In circles and into the abyss
Nothing makes sense in my mind
Just ignorant bliss

Just cutting my wrist, wishing they'd hear
My pain, it still exists
If no one listens, I cut deeper
Insanity knocks harder, persists

The shadows keep following me
Looking at me in the mirror
Tell them to leave the window to my soul
Leave the mirror… so I can see clearer

Written by: Casondra Nichole Austin

Carried Away

I get carried away by distractions

Trying to ease satisfaction

Always wanting to be right

Even if that means being impolite

Being non-productive

Or more like eternally destructive

Lies flow from the tongue

On drugs, sprung

All because I got carried away with distractions

Trying to ease satisfaction

Written by: Casondra Nichole Austin

Mending the broken pieces

Relief

Somewhere along the way

The game severely changed

Hopes and dreams splattered

Face and bones shattered

Who is that in the mirror?

Eyes dark with terror

Crushed beyond recognition

No dreams for a vision

Battered and bruised by many

Taken advantage of by plenty

No place to lay my head

Deceit to which I was led

Convinced I could do it on my own

Trying to remember what I had been shown

I set out to survive and win

Then broken once again

I finally threw up my hands

I had no more plans

Then I found relief

In God Whom I believe

Written by: Casondra Nichole Austin

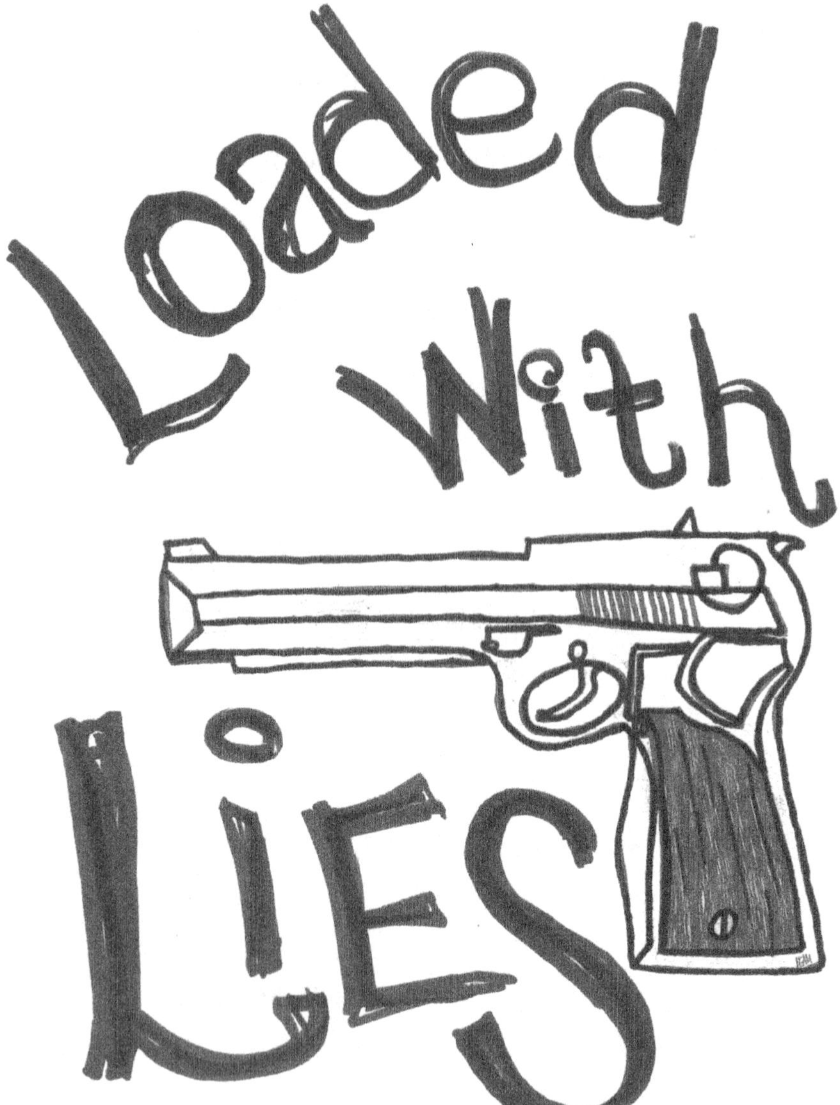
Loaded
With
Lies

Loaded Gun

Loaded gun, pull the trigger
Satan's lies, quick and slither

Fight hard this battleground
Please Lord, my mind, it's not sound

Send angels to ward them off
Use weapons far from soft

God, you say You've won this war
Why does the battle leave me tore?

Up and down, mountains and valleys
In Your book, are You keeping tally?

I want this life to be Your win
Then I turn again and sin

Forgive me, Lord, for all this havoc
Change this heart, forgive my tactic

Bless all the readers who heed
Help us all to believe

Written by: Casondra Nichole Austin

this mask is Tainted

Behind the Mask

Young and broken, full of pain

Tears and feelings, still this shame

How do I let out all this hurt?

When I don't know where to start

I have this mask, beautifully painted

But should I tell them it is tainted?

Fear of the unknown knocks on my door

It was so much easier to just be that whore

I'm trying so hard, yet it's still at bay

"You're getting better," I hear them say

I don't feel better, I just feel numb

I hide behind food and smiles, isn't that dumb?

I want to let it all out, let the tears fall

I know they will accept me, won't they all?

Trapped in this mask, I can't take it off

Lord please help me, make me soft.

Written by: Casondra Nichole Austin

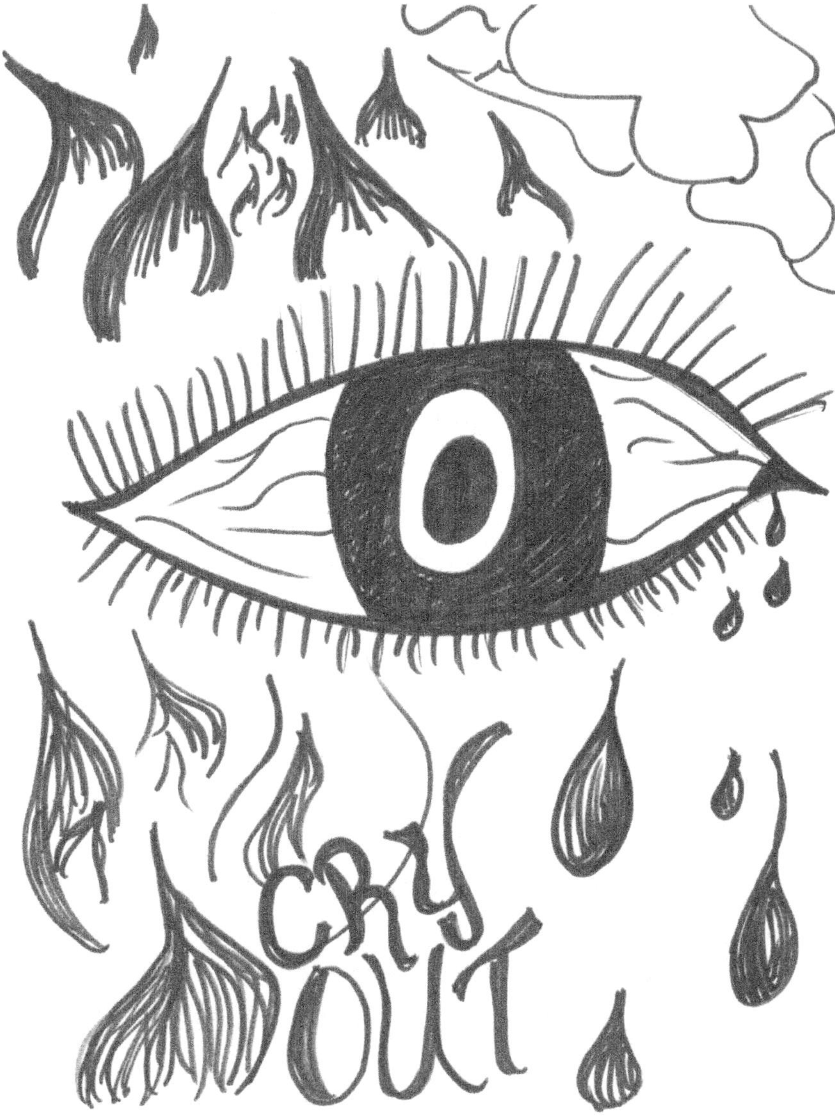
CRY
OUT

Crying Out

My soul cries out to the God of my heart
My sins never stop once they start

No ending to the hole I continue to dig
From evil words to taking a swig

I chase my pleasures, around we go
Satisfied by nothing, say it isn't so

My flesh fights and will hardly give
Begging for forgiveness, wanting to live

Yet I run in the wrong direction
Scared of change and of correction

My heart is explosive
I deeply wish I had pure motives

Last is first, and first is last
Love everyone and accept God's task

This war I wage within my soul
One day I'm on top, the next in a hole

My relationship with God will succeed
I know it's true, I do believe

Written by: Casondra Nichole Austin

I Will Show You

Why do I avoid these feelings?
While crying out for healing

I know if I keep Your commands
When I fall, on a cushion I will land

I'm desperately searching for who I am
In Your Word, it is found

Why, oh Lord, do I avoid opening?
The only chance I have at hoping

"Listen, Casondra, be still and hear
What's in your soul I'm trying to steer

I'm seeking intimacy to be your pleasure
For you, daughter, I have many treasures

My words, child, I don't want you to hide
that's what grows love, it amplifies

Surrender, daughter, is all I ask
And you will realize it's not just a task"

Written by: Casondra Nichole Austin

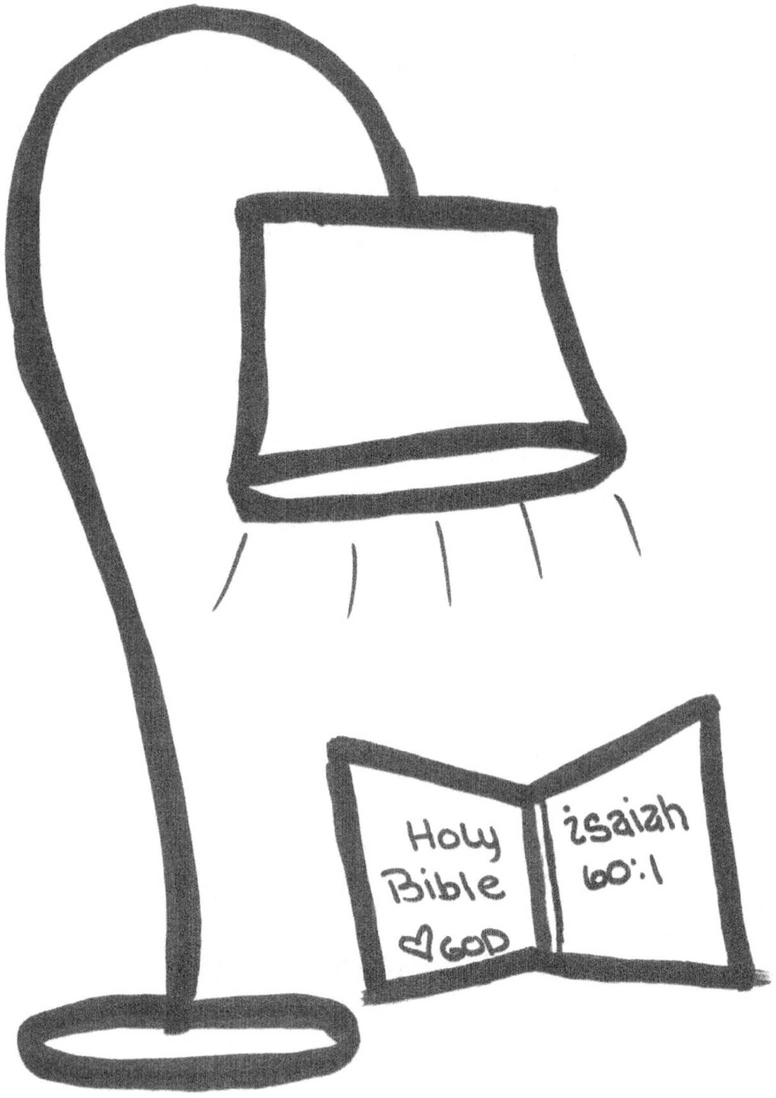
Holy
Bible
♡GOD
isaiah
60:1

Read

The mirror you use is jaded
Your view, My dear, is faded

Tainted has been your soul
Please open so you will know

I paid for you with a price
It was Me who gave My life

See how I have been patient and kind
I seek to renew your mind

I can't wait to see your eyes glisten
When the light comes on and you listen

Evil no longer has a grip
Living water, come, have a sip

Read what I have to say
There will be plenty of time to play

A clear view is ahead
Hold my hand as you are led

Written by: Casondra Nichole Austin

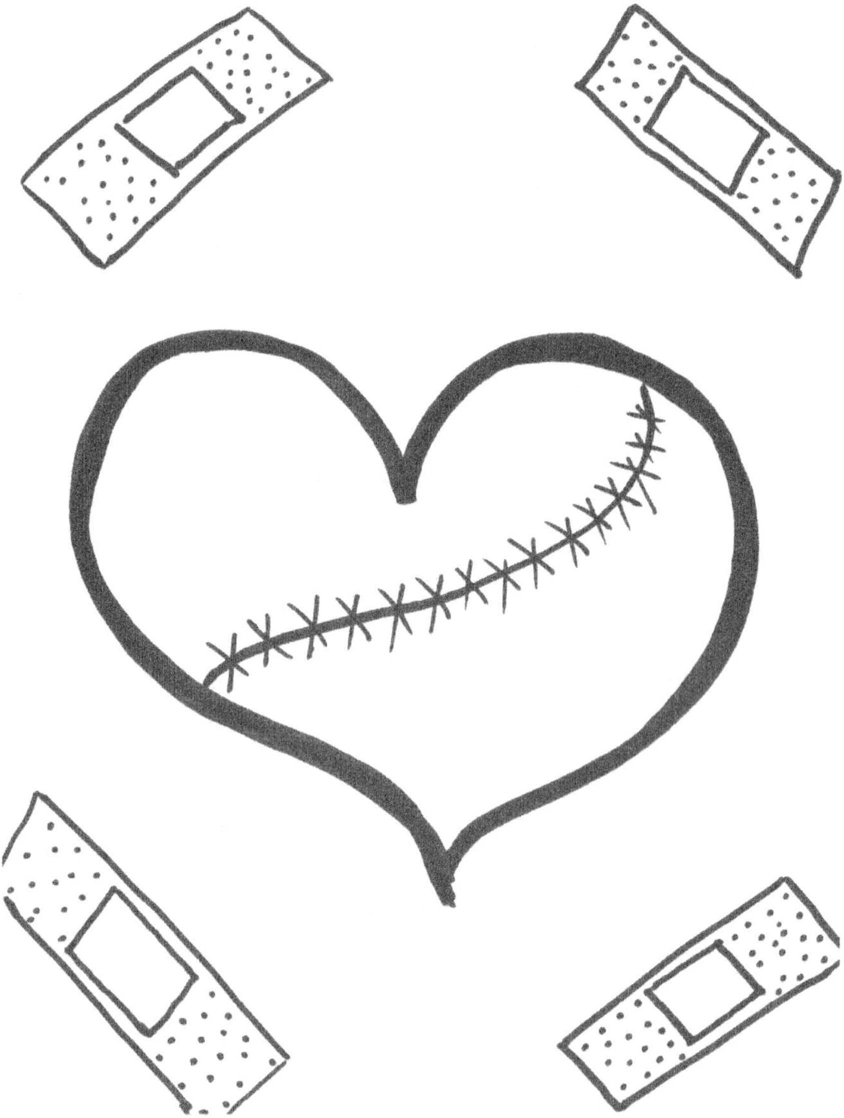

Healing

Tender love and care

Hurts to which I share

Twisted lies unravel

Kicking up this gravel

Classes, learning to live

My heart to God I give

Stronger upon time

As He renews my mind

Like a butterfly that He transforms

Healed from being scorn

Surrender, throw in the flag

For there is nothing left to hide

The process is painfully hard

As the cuts become scarred

But it's worth it each minute I grow

Not fast, just take it slow

Forgive and be forgiven

Learning a new way of living

Written by: Casondra Nichole Austin

Word of God

Word of God woo me in
Teach me of love, life, and sin

Penetrate my heart as I learn
Change my soul with each page I turn

Holy Spirit, lead, guide, and direct
Teach me all about the resurrect

Gluttony, greed, murder, and lust
Give up those things to You, Whom I trust

All through the Bible is one main theme
That my God sent Jesus to redeem

Body, mind, soul, and spirit
Open my eyes and ears so I can hear it.

Written by: Casondra Nichole Austin

WoO'd By ThE WoRd

Walk by Faith

To walk by faith and not by sight[1]

He's my shining armor, my knight

Never live your life in fear

Know always that God is near

Endurance to finish the race

Perseverance till you see God's face

Prayers and poems to your King

Listening to your best friend's sing

Contentment and peace He brings us

He always listens, never tells us to hush

When fear creeps in, He makes it go away

"Get behind me Satan"[2], He tells me to say

Love your neighbor as yourself

God will give us power, He will help

Holy Spirit He sends with peace and joy

A gift for all to accept.. mother, father, girl and boy

So walk by faith and not by sight[1]

Stay focused on God, day and night

Written by: Casondra Nichole Austin

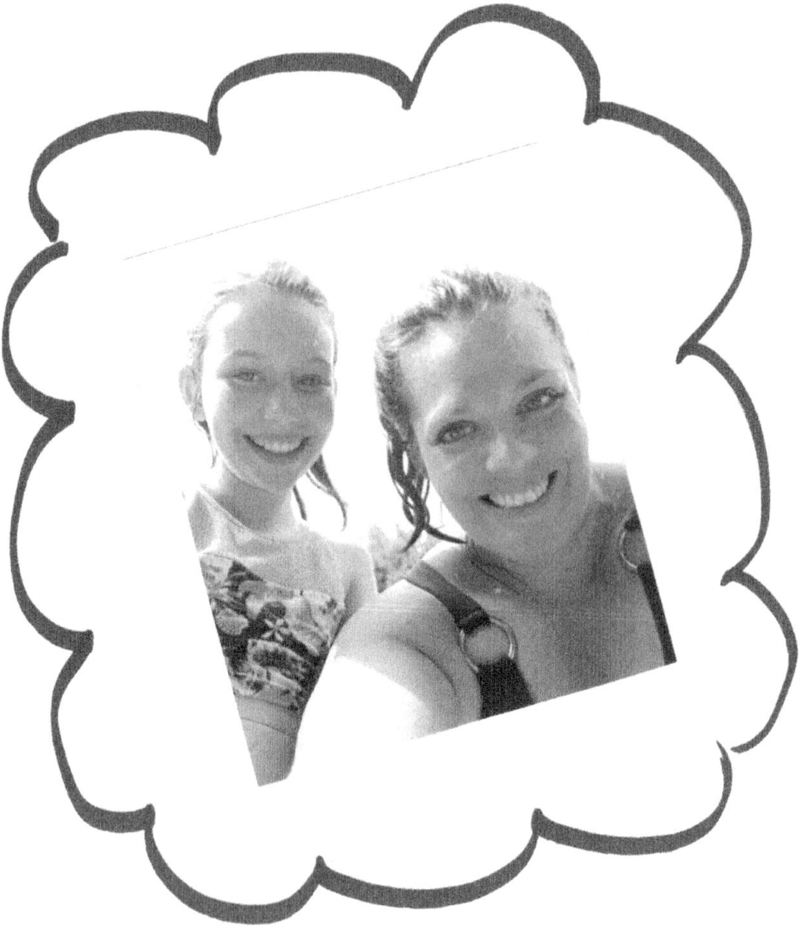

Mother's Day 2019

Mother's Day without your daughters
Unable to afford lawyers

Missing them so very much
Longing for their hands to touch

Do they miss or think of me?
Or do they resent, just wanting to be?

Do their new moms put flowers in their hair?
And watch Disney Channel, and sit in their little chair?

Do they chase them around the house?
And play still, quiet as a mouse?

Do they let them decorate their own cake?
And take them out to the lake?

Do they watch SpongeBob and Hannah Montana?
And write notes, pretending to be Santa?

Do they play dress up and straighten their hair?
Listen to music and let it blare?

Do they play games with them on their iPad?
I took for granted what I had

Once again I pray for a chance
To be their mom and take a stance

In their lives I want to be
But only if joy is what they will see

Written by: Casondra Nichole Austin

My Plans

JULY						2019
1	2	3	4	5	6	
7	8	9	10	11	12	13
14	15	16	17	18	19	20
21	22	23	24	25	26	27
28	29	30	31			

God's Hands

Much Greater

Lil' girl, hold tight, I have much in store
All your hopes and dreams, I'm about to open the door

You have suffered much pain, mostly because of your doing
But, lil' girl, know this, I never stopped wooing

See, I know the plans for your life, yes I the Lord
I give you the weapons to fight, I give you your sword

Now that you have returned to Me, and surrendered your device
Now, baby girl, I can give to you much more than you suffice

My plans are much greater, than you could ever hope
Just listen baby girl, I am better than dope.

Written by: Casondra Nichole Austin

i def. took 4 my family 4 granted... since Jesus broke the chains of slavery in my life, i have been blessed to see my mom, grandmom, + Zeta (my oldest daughter!!). i am still praying for an opportunity to see Zoey and Steelie (my middle and yaingest daughters) more importantly, i pray my family heals from the damage i caused! Please pray for them also! The power of prayer... blows my mind!

my God gives... and takes away... and as much as i truely want them apart of my life... i trust God to do what is best. Even if that means i cant be in thier lives... Let YOUR WILL BE DONE!

♡ casondra

Restore

Lord, please restore my family
From what Satan took
I walked down the wrong path
The bait... I bit the hook

But God You have redeemed me
The crooked You have made straight
That doesn't change the damage I have done
The "me" I caused them to hate

I am no longer the same woman
Open their hearts Lord, open their eyes
I'm not doing this for anyone else
But to have them would be a prize

However You choose to handle this Lord
I trust You to direct
Father, Your ways are the best
You have my utmost respect

Written by: Casondra Nichole Austin

Invade My Senses

Whispers of hope invade my senses

Dreams both big and small

Forgiveness from God so freely given

And passion so very tall.

A broken glass not long ago

Sharp and ready to slice

Then God put the pieces together

But His blood was the price.

Affection so pure that I cannot fathom

And love beyond all measures

The wonders and glory in His kingdom

Yet it's me that He treasures.

Written by: Casondra Nichole Austin

Brand New World

I look around and see my life
Peaceful and content.
Man this life is so much fun
Where has this year went?

I've worked through lots of pain
But still have more to go.
I'm grateful for the lessons learned
Though they seem so slow.

Take each day to the Lord
For it's His anyway
Thank you for this brand new girl
And that A Way Out is where I stay.

I am happy for each lady
That You have let me know
To stand beside through thick and thin
And care to watch me grow.

Here is filled with lots of love
Tears, joy and pain

Thank you for this brand new heart
And that I'm not the same.

Written by: Casondra Nichole Austin

God's Story of Redemption Through Kelsea Brooke Vaughn

For we do not have a High Priest who cannot sympathize with our weaknesses, but was in all points tempted as we are, yet without sin. Let us therefore come boldly to the throne of grace, that we may obtain mercy and find grace to help in time of need.

Hebrews 4:15-16 NKJV

Seek Him

When paint is dried on your broken heart
And deep within your soul, you are in tiny little parts . . .

Feelings of regret and abandonment sink in . . .
And you think to yourself, *"Where do I fit in?"*

When your mouth is on fire, but your mind is cold
You can never manage to remember what you were told

"What doesn't kill you makes you stronger", I'm beginning to believe
Look up. Seek God. He will help you to see

You're fanning flames no longer keep you warm
Being in the stillness of His presence is what comforts in your storm

It will quench your fire, wash away your stains
Give me comfort and peace, O Lord,
In Jesus' Name.

Written by: Kelsea Brooke Vaughn

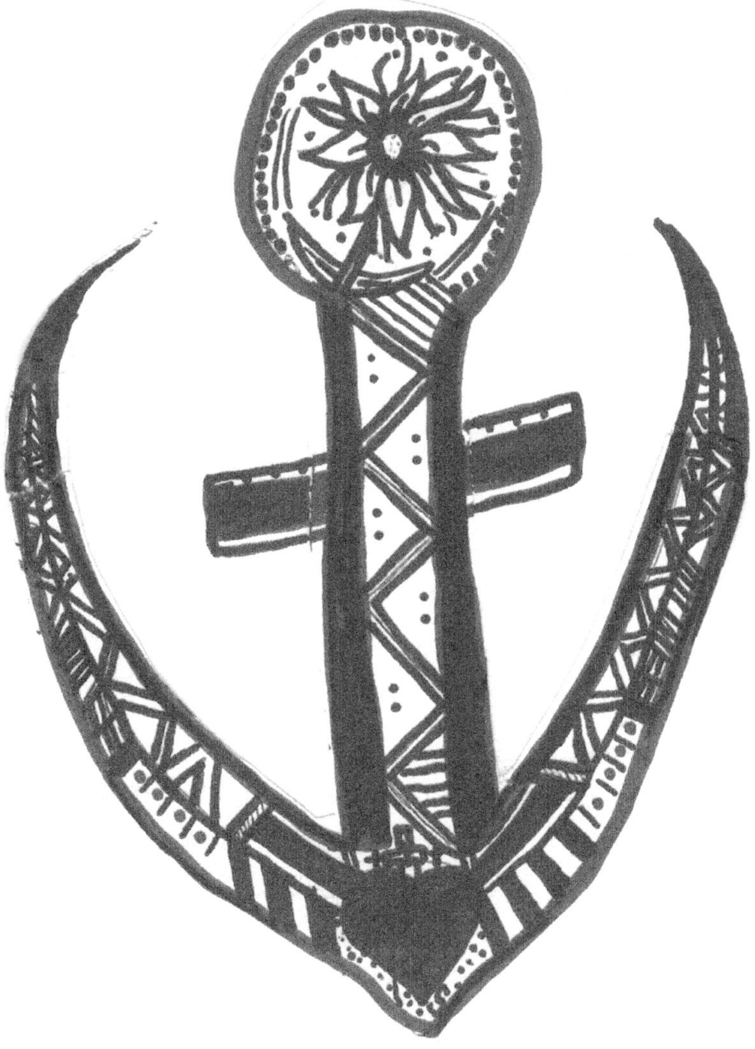

Refuse to Sink

Never turn around.
Never go back.
Keep your head up and stay on the right track.

It might seem impossible today
Have patience.
Be still and listen to what they say.

Your ears are flooded with Truth.
Float the wave and let it soothe.
Fight the wave? What's the use?

It is far too powerful and strong.
I refuse to sink. With God,
I won't be down too long.

He will have hold of me, on a tight rope.
My Lord Jesus will never forsake me.
A downward slope?

No.
Never again.
I have the Holy Spirit residing within.

A new and beautiful creation I am.
By the Grace of God the old me has died.

Glory be unto You, Father.
I am blessed, truly.
Savior, Healer, Deliverer, Messiah. My Lord Jesus Christ!
Without You, there is no life.

Amen!

Written by: Kelsea Brooke Vaughn

Invited

Invited are YOU into my imperfections
Out of this disastrous wreck I RISE
No longer broken sections

Mend me, My Mighty Father! Help me to win this fight!
In the mighty name of Jesus, Satan step down
You are no longer welcome here, for now, I have a crown

Through my faith and love
that can never be destroyed
My God overwhelms me with an unforgettable joy!

Chains are breaking. Burdens lifting.
Out of the darkness into His marvelous Light
Sweet and Holy One, I can only imagine the sight

Changed Forever
My Life . . .

Written by: Kelsea Brooke Vaughn

My

Life...

ChAnGeD

FoReVeR

God's Story of Redemption Through

Iris Socorro Santiago

The Lord is gracious and righteous; our God is compassionate. The Lord guards the inexperienced; I was helpless, and He saved me. Return to your rest, my soul, for the Lord has been good to you. For you, Lord, rescued me from death, my eyes from tears, my feet from stumbling. I will walk before the Lord in the land of the living.

Psalm 116:5-9, CSB

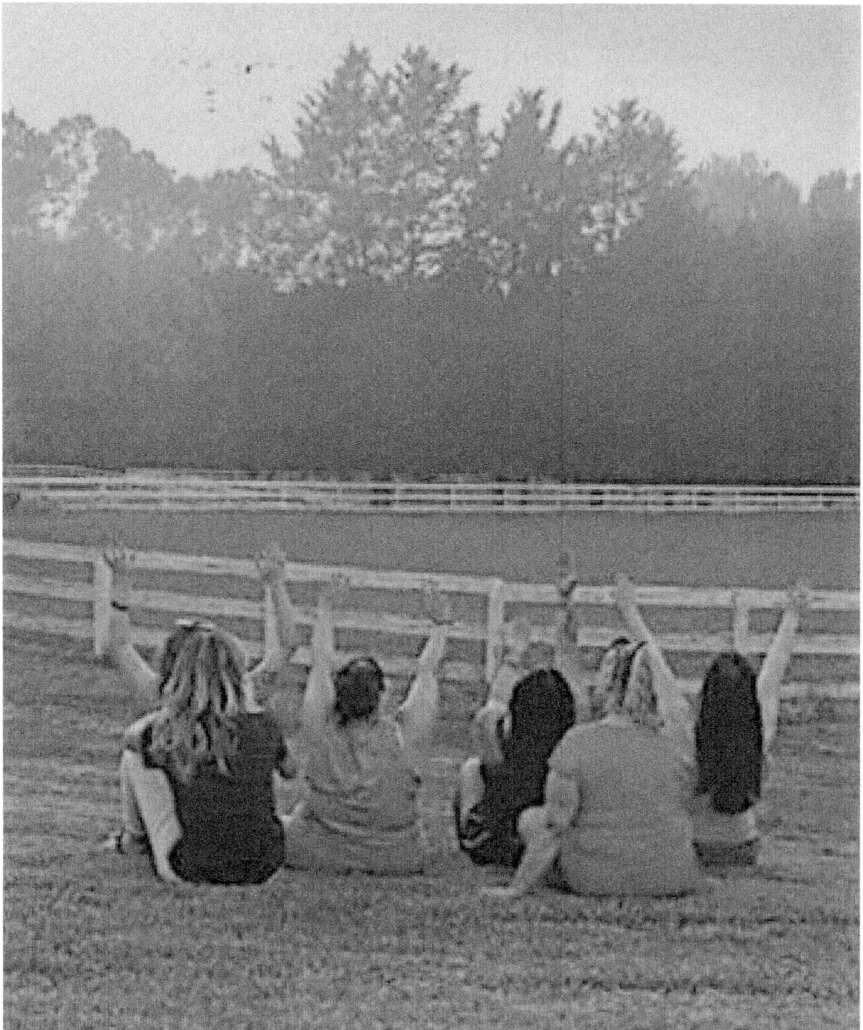

Reaching Out

God, I am trying. I'm reaching out
Do You hear my silent scream and shout?

I toss and turn late at night
Lord, it feels like I am falling apart

Keep me in Your sight
Lord, my wings are clipped, help me soar and take flight

Oh God, I'm tired and weak
Your voice I need to hear, so Lord speak

Your peace I desire
My soul You require

I know you are real, Jesus, I need to feel again,
my one and only friend

My Master, I am Your servant
Before You I bow and surrender
Jesus, be my Defender

Allow Your Truth to be my reality
Give me strength, perseverance, and tenacity

I'm empty inside, please, Lord, fill me up

Let my cup overflow,
I know You are big enough

Consume me, Jesus, I'm hurting inside.
Forgive me and teach me to let go
And let You be God

I'm weak, Lord, I need you to love me and change me
God, please show Your way.
Your truth. Your life.

God, I am trying to be more like You
and it's getting challenging
But I trust you and if I trust You
that means that You will continue to work in me

God I know that You are going to do great and mighty
things in my life
Please, Jesus, help me, to be better
I get off the throne so you can sit on it

I trust You to be King of my heart
Your kingdom is within me

Written by: Iris Socorro Santiago

I am Ready, Get Set, Let's Go

I am ready, get set, let's go
My heart fragmented, along with my wounded soul

Weary and burdened, tormented and scarred
I struggle to surrender complete control

Deliver me. I'm in bondage. I'm struck down.
These chains make me drop so low

Anger and pain
Russian roulette is a dangerous game.

Do I live or do I die?
If I choose life, please tell me why?

I'm crying out but it's a silent cry

When you look at me, what do you see?
A smile is what you see
But there's only fury inside of me

Oh my soul, you are not alone, He whispers
There is still time to save her.
I have not yet missed her

Time changes nothing. Yet, time changes all things
In life all things are not what they seem

Sorrow and misery have got to flee.
Yet they keep me shallow company

Everywhere I go, my baggage will follow
The more damage done, the more my heart feels hollow

I am forced to look up from this trauma.
Traumatic commotion
All of this is pointless drama

So much destruction has been done.
Abused and misused
When can I reveal the real me?

Hiding in my sin
Broken from within

Unveil me completely
Before the shadows consume me

911 this is an emergency
Come to my rescue
I'm half dead, half alive
Dear heaven, I need resurrection
I need life

I need the Love of Jesus Christ
to breathe
Heal me here and now

This dear God, is my broken hallelujah
Let me take a bow

You have saved me
And defeated the enemy

Amazing grace, how sweet the sound
I was lost but now I am found

I once was blind but now I see[3]
You, oh God, have predestined me
For such a time as this,

You called me out of darkness
Into your marvelous light
Not by my power or might
But by Your Spirit[4]

The pressure is on,
I can feel the pressing

Let the oil flow
Chosen and forgiven

Written by: Iris Socorro Santiago

1, 2, 3 Welcome to the Deep

Drug induced, physical abuse, and violated trauma
Submissive pain
That made me let go of the sun,
And yield to the rain

Dark seduction wrapped my soul,
Oh my weary soul
Burdened and heavy from all this shame
And control

Suicidal day and night
My mind insane, my heart in flight
Consumed and surrounded by darkness,
I saw no light

Struck down to the ground
No love, just hate
I looked death in the face
And took off her mask

Living in the land of bondage
I had no hope
Just a needle filled with numbness
And a scream stuck in my throat

A bottle of pills to disguise how I felt
I became a slave to the hand I was dealt

Victimized and tormented,
My heart was robbed of love
My soul was tainted, My spirit oppressed
By the heaviness in my chest

Every breath was my enemy
I tried to dance upon the heartache
For Christ's sake
But I lived my life like a mistake

I had no desire to live anymore
My heart became so weak,
My body was so sore

I have been undone by my sin
I am shackled from head to toe
In life you reap what you sow
I was brought very low

I had to look up
Forced to deal with this trauma
Alone with no daddy or momma
No one would save me

The flames surrounded me
Until I had an encounter with my master,
Jesus Christ

I yelled out, touch me I am as cold as ice
Far from nice

Save me with Your mighty right hand
Father God, nullify what the enemy had planned

Forgive me Jesus, deliver me and set me free
From these chains holding me
Open the prison doors,
Release me from this misery
What I need is real serenity

I need you to help me, I need a peace of mind
Father, my beloved, I'll let you catch me this time

Beauty for ashes[5], I shall rise up from the dust
With wings like eagles
Soar high above my situation
There is now no condemnation[6]

I am made new and made whole
I yield and surrender my soul
To You, Jesus
Hold me close and don't let me go

Jesus, Your perfect love casts out all fear[7]
You opened up my ears
And I hear Your voice say
"My child I will never let you go astray

You are in the Potter's Hands
You are the clay
Do not fear or be dismayed
Bind the strongman and turn from your ways

You shall know the truth and the truth shall set you free[9]
I am in control of Your destiny
No weapon formed by the enemy can stop Me

I am the LORD God Almighty

Call on My Name
Plead My precious Blood
And when the enemy comes in like a flood
I shall raise up a standard against him
Take the whole Armor of God and stand firm
Give Me your concerns

All that hinders must flee
You see,
I seek out My sheep

I never leave the one behind
I know you are still hurting deep inside

I was pierced for your transgressions[10]
I was crushed for your sins
And that punishment that brought you peace was upon Me
And by My wounds you are healed

I command My Word and it shall not return void
Peace be still, I am in your mist
Continue to call on My name
JESUS

I, my child, have never left you
With loving compassion I have drawn you to Myself"

It is the kindness of God that leads to repentance
Because of Your cross, Lord, there is no death sentence

Your salvation is my destination
Jesus, I made it through my test
Because You were there to carry me through my mess

I never could have made it without You
We overcome by the blood of the Lamb
and the word of our testimony[11]

God, I give You all the glory
My soul says *yes*
Use my mess and make it a message
Use my test and make it into Your testimony
of glory

Use my brokenness and make me a light
Today I stand united
with the Holy Spirit
Today is the day I fight

I declare and decree that
in my life I will see Your hand everywhere
Favor of God fall upon me

Open Your heavens, Heavenly Father
Rebuke the devourer
Place a hedge of protection all around me
Bind and confuse the enemy

I have faith to believe
I will see the goodness of the Lord
in the land of the living[12]

Strengthen me,
Anoint and preserve me for Your glory

Jesus, I bow before Your feet
And there I leave my crown
I hear the sound of chains falling,
You are my master
I surrender my broken alabaster.

Written by: Iris Socorro Santiago

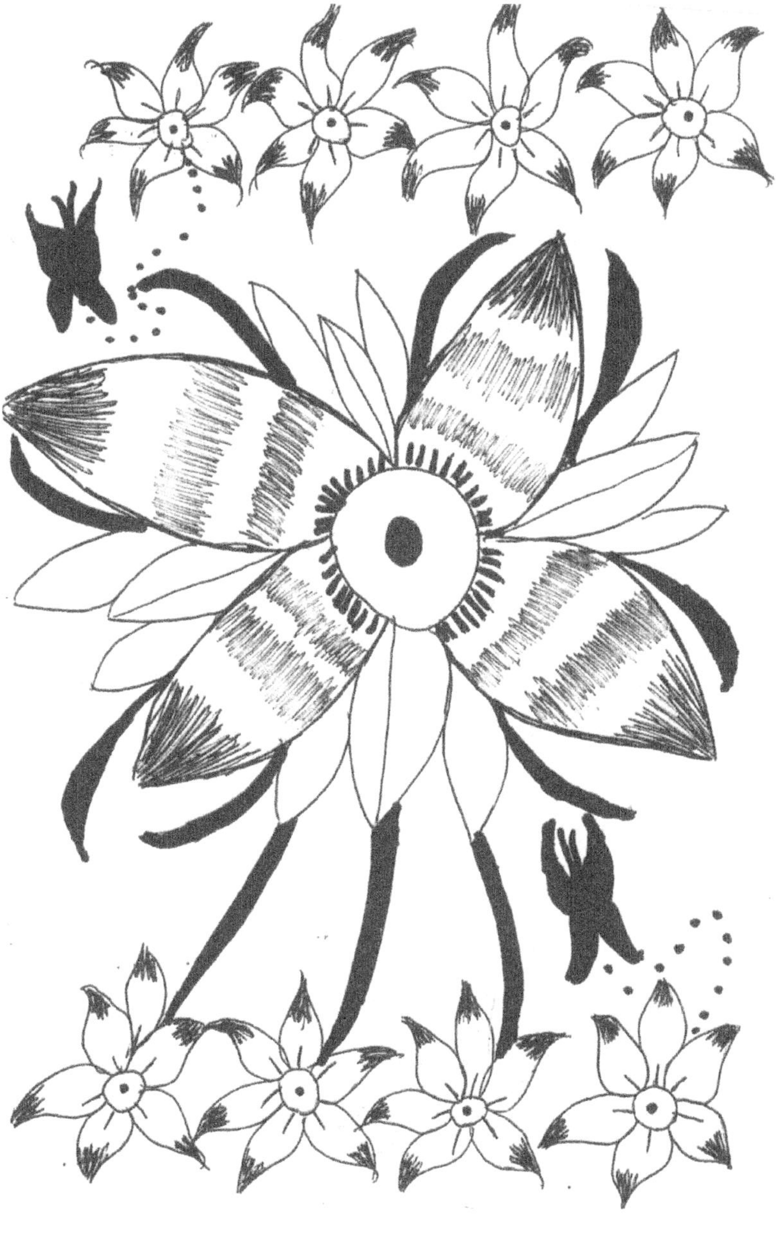

What Do You See?

When you look into my eyes, what do you see?

My child, I see the pain that you hide from me

The scars that don't fade

I see the brokenness of trust

I see the emptiness of love

I see you try to hide in the shadows

I see you bruised and I see you torn

But for such a time as this

You were born[13]

I created you in My image

I created you in pure love

Like a pretty white dove

I see you pure and I see you whole

I see what I can do through you

If you surrender your soul

I see what My will can be,

But I need to know.

Do you want to be set free?

You have to fight, you have to trust Me

I will never let you down,

I am faithful unto thee

I am on your side

And every tear you cry,

I hold in the palm of My Hands

For you Iris,

I have a plan

I know you by name

I call you and say

You will grow

And you will know

That I am the Lord your God

I will amaze you

And I will break you

I will change you

And make you know

My power and grace

You will seek Me

Face to face

And you will find Me

In a secret place

Written by: Iris Socorro Santiago

God's Story of Redemption Through Maria Claire

Be still, and know that I am God

Psalm 46:10, KJV

You intended
To harm
me, But
God
Intended
it for good...
Genesis 50:20a
(NIV)

Bitter Wounds

Bitter wounds
Bitter wounds
Yet,
I know Thou hast <u>NOT</u> forsaken me
Why?
Why do I run to self in times of distress?
So lonely there.
You are right here
EVERYWHERE
Yet,
I choose <u>NOT</u> seek
    Or speak
So lonely.
No feelings.
Yet,
The feelings weigh me down . . .
    They are all around!
PUSH THEM UP!
PUSH THEM OUT!
Have I the strength?
There they fly . . .
    Away . . .
Those heavy burdens.
    Bitter wounds.
Take them, Lord
    I see them in Your hands
Remolding
Give them back
Now healed in Your Love
Transforming

Floating back to me
Like clouds . . .

BLESSINGS!

Written by: Maria Claire

God's Story of Redemption Through Leah Gunn

We are hard pressed on every side, but not crushed; perplexed, but not in despair; persecuted, but not abandoned; struck down, but not destroyed.

2 Corinthians 4:8-9, NIV

HEAVY HAND

Cry out

For the oppressed

That have sunken into the pit,

And their faces let us not forget.

Cry out

For mercy upon the souls

Who live in deepest regret

That living under the heavy hand,

There, they found a place to fit.

Cry out

For those that despite

This reality

Live in total bliss –

WAKE UP!

Cry out

For the slave of the pimp's

Heavy hand.

Cry out

For the young women sold for little –

Yet high is the demand.

Cry out

For the daughters

Who ran to the streets alone –

The ones who could not

Lay their heads

Safely in their homes.

Cry out

To our Creator

For He sits upon

His throne.

LORD, bring these women to

The TRUTH that they are not alone!

Cry out

For the souls

Walking the streets –

That they will be

Made known.

Cry out

In prayer

That the Father's power

In all their lives be shown.

Cry out

For the Gospel

THAT WILL LEAD TO STREETS OF GOLD.

Written by: Leah Gunn

TREADING the GREY

TEARS OF TERROR

My cry came out in countless ways

Not once or twice, but countless days.

I cursed - I stole - I mocked - I strolled -

Yet my secrets I never told.

The pain ushered me down the darkest road.

I shifted the blame-

Switched my role.

It had to be my fault

Of that thought I couldn't let go!

In survival mode.

Now looking into the mirror

I feel my heart go cold.

Tears of terror

- lines of coke -

I'm waiting for the drain.

I cry out to God once again,

Then hold my head

In shame.

1-2-3

Pump my fist…

Searching for a vein.

Oh, what a messy web - I can't be loosed.

There's no hope

I can sustain.

Forgive me, Lord,

My prayers

Protect my sin

So peace

I can't obtain.

Without this dope, I cannot cope

And lessen all this pain.

It saves me from grieving the loss

Of my dignity

The reality leaves me

DRAINED.

Everyone looking from the outside in,

Quick to label me

INSANE

To do it over and over again

- same result -

DISDAIN.

A small still frame.

A scar on my arm -

Lasting mark on my name.

Snap back

To myself

Look into the mirror

I daze……

Crying, *JESUS!!!*

Is there any hope

That such memories

You can erase?

Intercede for me!

I'm lost in a

Mindless matter.

Sinking from 50 cc's and

Then the blood, it splattered.

Loose the tourniquet from my sleeve-

I feel the breath

Then stall…Cry out to my reflection,

When will you at last fall?

I reach out

For death….

Please take away your grip

Away from my secrets slip

And be freed from all of this.

LEAH

Written by: Leah Gunn

INNOCENCE

SO PRECIOUS

SO PRICELE$$

YET SO

EXPENSIVE.

WRONG TIME - WRONG PLACE

I came up with a different frame of mind
Than those who accompanied my space.
I found the silver lining in the darkest of greys.

As time pressed on,
I was looking at pure evil
Day to day.

Hidden in plain sight
Without a trace,
Incognito to a gaze .

No matter how hard I tried
I couldn't make the pain go away.
My innocence was betrayed.
No matter how I tried, I couldn't make the grade.

No deed done was good enough to meet
The demands and
Stop the craze.

Wounds surfaced and scarred
As violence snuffed out the love ,
No longer leaving any space.

Trying to hide my feelings towards my situation

I laughed and spoke
With a hasty pace.

But the truth was evident on my face.
Black and blue eyes
With cuts of rage.

Life of trials -
Submerged
In God's grace.

Every day I put on a charade.
Scapegoat for the masses
I took it all on my plate.
A heavy load for a young girl
Who had yet to see a date.

I endured the worst abuse one could imagine
In their dark embrace.

Confused as to what exactly the details were
Against me in their case?

Why was I finding myself
The center of such distaste?
One used for pleasure amidst their pain –

Pruned and prodded
I became a stewardess of lies

An escape.

And make no waves.

I became a product of what I endured
And the worker of sinful estates.

The guilt of my own compliance
Left my soul
In a guilt ridden haze.

The Lord could never forgive one such as myself,
I cried
Grabbing a suitcase.

In so much haste
Running from the history
Of this complicated debate.

TRUTH versus lies.

Self versus the enemy
in disguise.

Exhausted I cry

"Lord, show me the truth
And give me a way out of this life….

Away from those who've lead me astray.

So many years have passed
So many days.

I need you to help me God.
I have been running from your face-
Out of shame and disgrace."

THEN

The Lord sent a couple
To pick me up
And share the truth in love.

The lady, she was sweet, sincere,
And gave the softest hug.

The man, a preacher,
Who I know to this day
Was sent from God above
He pulled over,
He asked a simple question,
"If you died today,
Would you go to heaven?"
I shrugged,
And gave a confused expression.
I don't know,
I have been labeled a hellion.

Living as a prostitute
Running in rebellion.

The rest is history
And this is my story
Of redemption.

The Lord heard my prayer
And today
I write free of condemnation,
And can say in confidence
I have found true Salvation.

I found the Lord in the parking lot of a gas station.

Thank you, Lord, for A Way Out-
I give you a standing ovation!

Written by: Leah Gunn

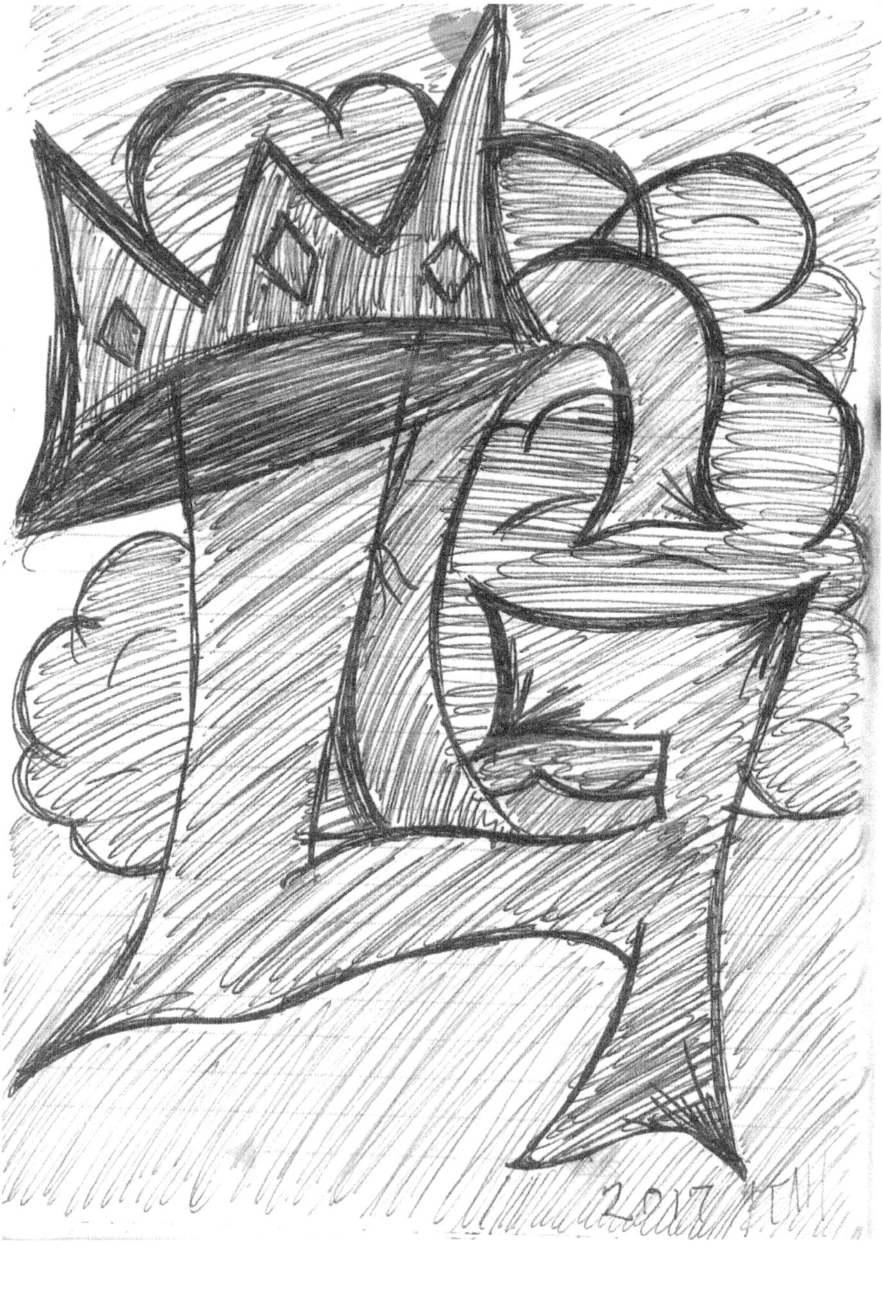

MY SPREE

I CAN'T BELIEVE

I HAD GIVEN UP ON LIFE

LIKE IT WAS NEVER MEANT TO BE.

RUNNIN A RAT RACE WITH NO FINISH LINE

-LOOKING TO SUCCEED-

AT FEELING BETTER ABOUT MYSELF

TO EVEN THE SMALLEST OF DEGREE.

I STUFFED MY FLESH FULL OF IT'S DEMANDS

BUT TO NO AVAIL THIS SPREE

- WITH OR WITHOUT-

NEVER SATISFIED

-WITH OR WITHOUT-

NEVER FREE.

HEAL ME, JESUS, SAVE MY SOUL?

I'M BEGGING YOU AND I DECREE,

"NO LONGER WILL I GO ON LIKE THIS-

AT LAST,

I'M DONE -YOU'LL SEE."

I PRAY WHEN YOU LOOK

D

O

W

N

FROM HEAVEN YOU'LL SEE

A

Little

piece

of

You

in

me.

Written by: LEAH

My bunk is hard

The only color that I see
Is of the beautiful cards for me.
It hurts to say not one I see
Is from outside of my family tree.

So where are you?
There's no need for further proof to see
That your far from me-

PAIN
A common word that goes through my mind-
Then, "Dear sweet Jesus,
How long have I been blind"?

I'm awakened now
Where do I pick up from?

There's no room for error,
This try is my last one.

As long as I look back,

I see where all my opportunities have gone.

NEED

I need to be free

Yet have some boundaries.

I need lines drawn in the sand

That will save me from ruining me-

I'M TIRED

Tired of acting out this ongoing play

Like all of my reality won't

Come crashing in on me one day.

MY BUNK IS HARD

The lights are bright

No one see's my tears at night.

I scream,

I try to justify the things I've done

My insides cry.

I need success

And nothing less

No excuses like stressed, depressed

Now I'm obsessed with betterment.

Whether I succeed -or whether I fall

My efforts

D

R

O

P

Me off here guarded behind brick walls.

Before I'm allowed to rest

I must

~GO~

TELL ALL WHO WILL LISTEN

OF THE ONE AND ONLY SAVIOR

AND TELL THEM I'M A CHRISTIAN.

Only now before I Rest

I must complete this mission

And scream from the roof top "ALL MY SINS THEY WERE FORGIVEN".

So for all of those

Who left me all alone in my prison

A pretty card can't compare

To the present

That I was given

And that's.. my new life.

Written by: Leah Gunn

TOE TO TOE

The pain, the regret, my need to be free.
What do they see
When they look at me?

So many things I've done-
Countless as the sand on the shore of the sea.
Fighting this demon of addiction
Toe to toe,
In a boxing ring.

Take a deep breath
- Ball my fists -
Roll up my sleeves.

Who I was-
Is no longer
Who I aspire to be.

This war amidst my members
A battle to the death.
The true score
No one's counting
But me.

Round 2.
Will there be a round 3?

Limited choices are laid out in front of me.

Locked up- covered up- sobered up
Which will it be?
Time will tell
Then someone will know
Other than me.

Written by: Leah Gunn

CHOSEN

Heavenly Hope

Sing praises of protection

Oh my soul!

For God will

Redeem, replenish

And make me whole.

Remembrance

that

He laid down His life -

Sacrificing His own.

Helped I am by this truth

That when He calls,

I have a

HEAVENLY HOME

He took a last breath,

Now awaits

At the right side of the throne.

Oh the trouble

That shadows my call.

A stranger's voice is calling

But

For the grace of God

I shall not go!

Under the pressure

Or the power of my foe

A desperate prayer drops me to the floor.

In the Word

On my knees

I find freedom from

Oppression –

The enemies control.

In the midst of this battle,

I cry aloud

NO!

I'm a child of God

I have a heavenly hope.

Written by: LEAH

PAY

HIM

HIS

DUE

IN

DEED

INDEED

INDEED

Today you set me free!

Today You answered my prayer

And worry released

As I prayed for mercy from the grief –

You blessed me.

My thoughts - my plans, could not compete.

A short sighted inclination of the path that,

You only,

Could upkeep.

Until the fullness of Your power would sow,

Refreshing my soul

I weep

"God, is this the pain that has rendered me at a loss?

Living in total defeat?"

I can't see!

Without your gracious provision of revelation

I shall not reap.

Oh how the depths of darkness have lost their grip on me!

In the reality of

Your continuous control

over-

EVERYTHING!

One day my transformation will bring glory to my King!

Look over the pit and deepest valley beneath -

There was **no devil in Hell**

That could thwart predestiny!

Ordained and chosen,

A vessel for good use –

Not one of dishonor

Amidst the heap.

A stranger's voice cannot call any longer,

Or gain any heed.

For I am filled with the ultimate authority

Of Jesus Christ's power –

He is the Good Shepherd;

My soul,

His sheep.

What a joyful noise I'll make at Heaven's gate

When I see ~my God!

GLORY TO THE HIGHEST!

PAY HIM HIS PRAISE,

FOR IT IS DUE

IN DEED.

Written by: Leah Gunn

THE HEIST

What a blessing this couple can be!
The face of friendly and kind to see.
Fun, outgoing, loving, and inspiring to me.

They opened their hearts and then followed mine.
They make me grateful I survived.
I was almost robbed of all the goodness of life.
Then the HEIST.

A robbery of the belief that I was all alone.
As I carried a broken heart, oh so far from home.

They shared their wisdom, time and love,
So fortunate I feel– an answered prayer from above.
I feel such joy.
This has been a gift that I could only dream of.

I tell you it has changed my life since I met these two.
A fitting last name, for they stole my heart and
Changed my thoughts
Of what was real and true.

People do care?!
WHO KNEW!
It's as if the days we have spent
Have washed my eyes anew.

I can see all the possibilities for my life,
And believe they can come true.
Together, as friends,
We talk about a new journey
And how far I have to come, too.

I enjoy watching them do life
And they help me push on through.
I have a support system. New goals
And I'm in pursuit.

A SPECIAL THANKS FOR THE HEIST
THAT HELPED MY HEALING COME TRUE.
YOU STOLE AWAY THE BURN OF DEFEAT
AND HELPED THE LIGHT COME THROUGH.

Written by: Leah Gunn

Doing Life

The tale of a God given friendship and redemption.
The Mission:
To highlight the power of God's intervention.

Once upon a time, there was a woman
Who fell into darkness and confusion.
The days came in a haze
And nights filled with rage.
The pain so evident of her intoxicated face.

She cried out to the Lord
And her cries He heard.
The loneliness of addiction
Left her solitude on the curb.

Then the Lord sent her help from above.
The "A Way Out" Program
The avenue to Him that He preferred.
As the Holy Spirit cleansed her
From all her dirt.

Now what to do about her mind?
Due to abuse –
Her beliefs about friendship
Had been obscured.

A mentorship was the order
Which was chosen by the Lord.
The prescription – a woman name Theresa –
Who as Jesus' hands and feet did serve.

Such a beautiful woman to come and help carry the
Burdens of Leah – her new charge.
A God-given friend who He could use
To guide
And stand by her side.

Bringing the realization of what life could be
If only she would push through the fire.
The days were full of laughter
And prayers for new desires.

Affirmation came from Theresa
And new dreams she inspired.
The words of encouragement
Helped Leah to look higher!

The standards had been raised and seeds of hope
Been sown.
The most comforting of all
Was that Leah would not be doing life.
Alone.

They stood together in battle
And prayed for God's will.

They rebuked the lies of the enemy
And stood on truth
To be still.

They shared their stories of the days
When sin in their lives had reigned.
They cried; they laughed at loss and gain –
Finding freedom even in pain.

The truth had set them free
And lies set them apart –
For the Lord in His cleansing grace
Made them together – a work of art.

By two I send you out, says the Lord –
You're not to be alone.
I'll give you strength to fight this battle together –
Until I bring ya'll home.

Both mentor and mentee believed
Who God said they were
And what He claims as true,
But until the Lord brought them together
This mentee never knew
Just how much
She could truly do.

Today, I thank God for this tale of friendship
And of hope!

I give thanks to God for my mentor
Who has helped me on my journey
To succeed and cope.

Glory to God for answering my prayer
From a friendless deep dark pit.
He brought me out to see the love of a true friend –
And find my hope
In Him.

Theresa is a vessel
Who the Lord so mightily used.
She puts her own pain aside
To make the best of His good news.

Her heart is so big and smile so wide –
As she walks with me through life.
I'm so grateful for the support she gives
And so blessed that with her
I take all the days in stride.

This happy ending
For such a sad beginning
Makes me so grateful
Because it makes God known!
Such a tale as this
Could only be from God alone.

Written by: Leah Gunn

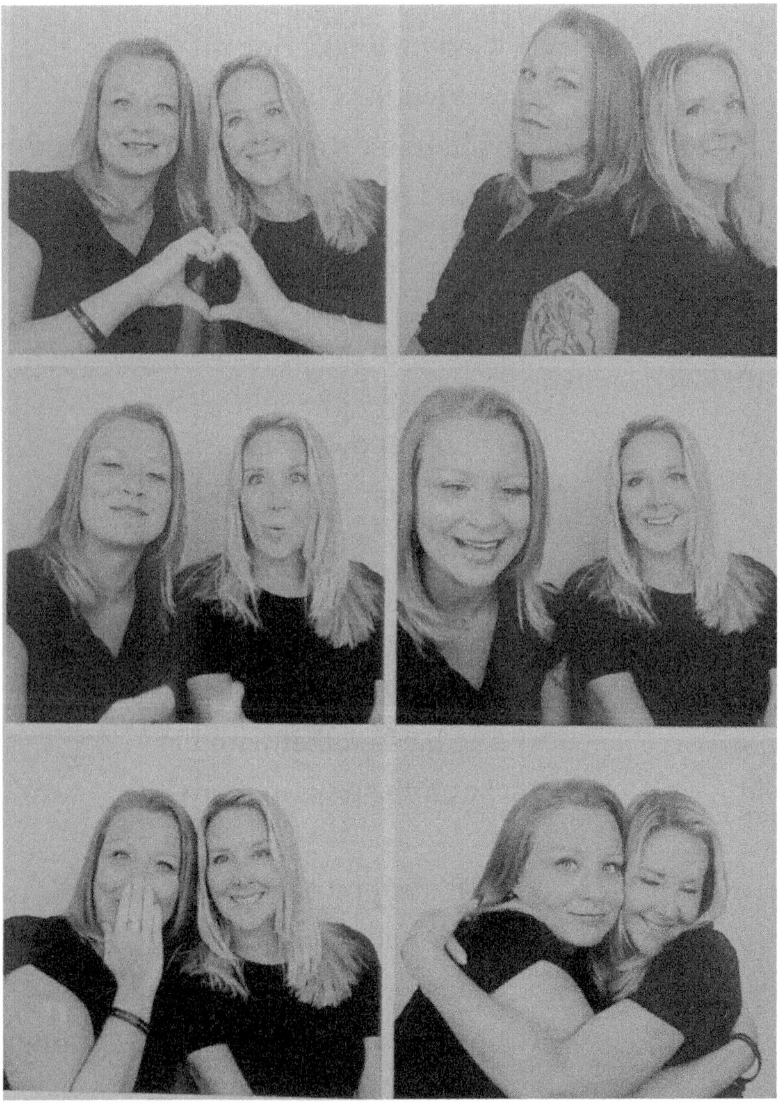

YOU GOTTA HATE THAT SIN

Mrs. Carol Wiley, my counselor, teacher and friend

Can be found in those feared dark places

Where my story begins.

She found me in many chains

Where many lies I had believed.

She spoke to me about the Lord

And about his Holy Spirit who was grieved.

She taught me about grace

And who I am in Him.

She taught me he wasn't a "Get you God"

Instead he is a friend.

She taught me about reverence

And bowing to a Holy God.

She taught me about my dignity

That no one should disregard.

NOT EVEN ME

She taught me black and white truth

And how to call it out.

She taught me how to live a life of faith

Resisting fear and doubt.

She hates the sin that so easily entangles

And against it she speaks out.

"YOU GOTTA HATE THAT SIN!"

She says with a godly heartfelt shout.

You gotta hate that sin

To keep you from going back

To where God has called you out.

Thank you God for A Way Out!

I praise God for Mrs. Carol and for her life's work.

My heart is so filled with gratitude

To know her here on earth.

Thank you so much Mrs. Carol

For believing I could change.

Thank you for all the help you have given

and your work in JESUS name.

Written by: Leah Gunn

Casondra Austin

Survivor since June 25, 2018

Kelsea Vaughn

Survivor since March 25, 2019

Maria Claire

Survivor since March 5, 2018

Iris Santiago

Survivor since January 23, 2019

Leah Gunn

Survivor since September 6, 2018

Made in the USA
Middletown, DE
22 May 2021